D1713211

Noble Gas,
Penny Black

Noble Gas,
Penny Black

David O'Meara

Brick Books

Library and Archives Canada Cataloguing in Publication

O'Meara, David, 1968-
    Noble gas, penny black : poems / David O'Meara.

Poems.
ISBN 978-1-894078-68-9

I. Title.
PS8579.M359N62 2008   C811'.54   C2008-903161-X

We acknowledge the Canada Council for the Arts, the Government of
Canada through the Book Publishing Industry Development Program
(BPIDP), and the Ontario Arts Council for their support of our
publishing program.

 Canada Council   Conseil des Arts   Canada   ONTARIO ARTS COUNCIL
for the Arts   du Canada   CONSEIL DES ARTS DE L'ONTARIO

Cover photo: "Nontitled" (from White Lines series), 2003, by James Erdeg.

Edited for the press by Henry Shukman.

Author photo: Jim Bryson.

The book is set in Minion and Frutiger.

Design and layout by Alan Siu.

Printed and bound by Sunville Printco Inc.

Brick Books
431 Boler Road, Box 20081
London, Ontario N6K 4G6

www.brickbooks.ca

For Dorothy

CONTENTS

I

II

III

I

The Next Day

You turned forty all afternoon,
and with every hour's drink you poured,
you aged. The thought was fuel; your mind roared
like a fire, like a starved sun

eating its core, making a feast
of the fears that remained. But the next day arrived,
and you were safe, and sane; not in the least
surprised you'd lived.

Station

The sandwich was crap, the tea
magnificent in the café
of the Ankara Central, its massive

girdered roof spanning the platform
and greased tracks, grimed black
by an industrial century or two,

the air all Bogart
with smoke and goodbyes.
Waiters in dark trousers and bowties,

the kettle's aluminium whistle, whiffs
of coal, and the toilet attendant's
wrinkled gaze

each in their separate turns
received us for that hour of delay
arranged below the heavy hands

of the big, iron clock. Forced to wait,
I watched your face, freckled by sun,
still holding an afterglow

of southern coast, where our thoughts
had been gently rocked through a stretch
of good weather, days

which claimed nothing, just lent
themselves with grace, felt
but never held, like wind over water.

Travel

Arriving here, across the blue sheet
at the inside of your thigh:
that supple groove, where muscle and tendon
pool into the polished dimple
near your torso, moon-white
but glazed with sweat,
like a celadon finger-bowl.
Later, I dream of the edges
of warm and cold fronts—those curved, tensile
lines on weather maps—and what
they represent. The patient heat,
shook-tin sky, the erotic suspense
of fields below thunder.

Sick Day

The year's near done
and a buttery pad of sun
slides below the slanted roofs.
The window
strobes our life at passing cars.

You've been wrapped
in a heady cloud of antiphlogistine,
goose down, and humidifier steam;
your slick hot brow

now pulses against my palm
in the diurnal twilight
of our bedroom. *Are you ok?*
There's a click of lozenge
against your teeth, a coughed, lemon pause
until your voice creaks

like a breathy hinge
through a smile. *Bunny,*
I'm not feeling well.
I'll stay home too, make soup
against your temperature's flux,
putter through

the hours, our see-saw evening
of crosswords, photographs, question
marks on next year's calendar
as the ploughs scrape skeins

of snow toward the buried curb.
We talk past midnight. Quilt-folds
pocket a splay of warmth, hold
the fever before it breaks
in sleep, against the laundered sheet, my
arm, and your book of mysteries.

Charlotte St.

So much the same, we fight to be different,
facing the close walls of this dark apartment
on Charlotte Street. The dry, white day
is draped outside our kitchen window,
where a tree rattles, bare as a coat hanger.
We're sad but willing to believe all the rumours
of a simple spring. The cold-encased street,
the slush-messy street, the snowy street…
Two more weeks to another insufficient paycheque,
our patience cracking like an ice pack;
then up half the night laughing, the last
kids with the lights left on.
How fast a month goes when you can't make rent,
how mean the restaurants look, how hard
everything seems, remembering fun
but too stretched to share it.
I'll wait, and wait, and walk with you endlessly.
Let's ditch this city, these jobs, all the bother
of having things, and keep only each other.

Airport

The roughest takeoff from the airport
could never outdo the shock of parting.
There I was, buckled in, frightened
like a child, not from safety
instructions, or the engine-drone starting,

but your figure waving
behind the glass of the observation deck,
though you couldn't have guessed I was watching.
And also couldn't see me waving back
the whole runway's length, even after your solitary speck

was lost. Then the further auctioning off
of towns and hills that flashed below—going, gone
as I left the coast behind. I turned
my head away, shut my eyes. It wasn't, but felt
like the saddest thing I've done.

Tales from the Revolution

It's Christmas, 1958, and is there anything
sexier than Cuba? Errol Flynn, faded swashbuckler, bloated
from a floating

decade of vodka, bent spoons, and hypodermics, steers
his white convertible—Havana to Santiago—through the central
battle sectors

of the revolution. He's here to shoot his latest feature, *Cuban
Rebel Girls*, starring ingénue Beverly Aadland, seventeen, thin
and green as cane,

playing the young American in love with a rebel
fighter. Flynn will appear as himself. There's a spot to park back
of the hotel,

so they dock the car, then ask around for Castro. He's here,
turns out, across town, in a room at the Central America, digesting
the better share

of a festive meal of turkey, black beans, rice, and a cup of mud-
black coffee. Past midnight, a message comes. "Who?" "You know…
Robin Hood, Don Juan, Captain Blood."

—◇◇◇—

The last minutes of December. Casinos
and nightclubs boom with Big Bands and high-stakes swagger.
Lucky Luciano,

capo de tutti capi, from a high window verging on the Newest Year,
admires the waves' blunt force rushing the rails of the Malecón.
He's here

for the fireworks show, and to toast the last heyday of a gangster era
when the mob-boss delegates paid him homage, when the honeymoon
of Frank and Ava

shared the self-same atmosphere with Disney, Astaire, and the tobacco reek
of Churchill's pout reflected off the Nacional's tiled lobby.
But now the break

is coming as Batista arrives, across town, late to his own private
party. Glum, he eats dinner where he's standing, clears his throat
as the date

ticks to the first stark minute of '59. Already back
in the presidential suite, his children clutch their stamped visas; the DC-4
is fuelling on the tarmac,

waiting on the hurt, defiant speeches of another violent shift of power.
His guests' leather shoes creak. He's here to say they have
one hour

to pack and join him as he slips through the noose of history.
Now there's a jangling of telephones in Miramar, high-heel
staccato and teary

gasps down the halls, a collective rummage for money and jewels. Those
with no time to change, arrive at the customs counter
still in gowns and tuxedos.

—⚉—

8 a.m., January 1st.
Edwin Tetlow, British correspondent, is startled awake by a sudden
unmistakeable burst

of silence. "He's just gone
with the night," his assistant blurts. Who? "You know. Batista. El Presidente."
Along the Malecón

nothing moves; no resident, police
or soldier, and the painted shutters of the shops are closed.
Tetlow eyes

his Underwood, its work-rubbed keys.
He's here to finesse the reports of troops, chaos at the desks
of foreign embassies

with the sound of news coming off the wire.
The letters clack against their rollers, predictable as the rush of surf,
as Hollywood, or gunfire.

All-Inclusive

Our white skin won't bronze. Since autumn, we've lumbered
through the slush, ice and cold, so our resistant limbs now bared
to a genuine sun seem even whiter; then the first scorched dab
of red appears, like a gypsy bauble, on my unprotected earlobe.

Through the provinces, reality nudges … carpool depots
where schoolkids and labourers watch blankly as our charter-bus slows
but passes, stately and exempt as any government official, northwards
through the unlit streets of Santa Clara. The ageing patriarch, on billboards,

still in olive battledress, assures *Vamos Bien*, backing his wager
with Venezuelan oil and the market for tourism and cane sugar.
Red flags spike the sand, a warning to swimmers. We wade
dumbly in; the reversing surf slaps us flat, our only reward

some crotch sand and a mouthful of salt water. I hardly care,
selfish, facing the lazy pose of you stretched on a beach chair,
while back in our room, on cable, worlds teeter at the brink, borne
along on the staged climaxes of disaster movies and soft porn.

This Age
– after Ahkmatova

Why are things worse than they've ever been?
Sometimes, distracted by the mind's great grief,
we'd lop our own hand off to stop the pain,
then fidget with the stump so there's never relief.

In the west the pretty sun reddens like a grindstone
and scatters its sparks till the clustered rooftops shine;
but there, in bold crosses, Death flags each door with chalk
for the ravens, and the ravens won't bother to knock.

Czarna Polewka

When he crossed the valley
and frozen creek bed, he could hear
a curt squeal of shifting ice,
and the chop of wet-packed snow.

An hour across, the chatter
of home still in his ears. A reproachful
whinny strained from the saws
of his father's lumberyard.

But the return was all moon, his
veil of breath and the hacked-out
silhouettes of spruce. Then the view
towards his life, and no good

news to take there;
only the warm, black stone
of his stomach,
the taste of duck blood and plum.

Black Soup. In Polish folklore, this was traditionally served to young suitors if
the parents of the intended bride had decided to reject his proposal.

Nothing

"Nothing," he said, "it's nothing."
Then nothing was said. Silence; nothing.

What she asked had come from nothing.
Sweet nothing, really, was all he said.

They cut their links like little wires, said
nothing about it afterward, nothing.

All over nothing.
So never to talk of what they said

until all that was ever said
was nothing, and so nothing was ever said.

Night Train

With the parents and their child, we were five
in the sleeping car, the scoured steel rails
shunting us further into Asia.

You and I stared at nothing, just the coming dark,
then watched the father, by cabin light,
turn the pages of our guidebook

until his finger with its calloused whorls floated,
slowed and stalled above one town. "Nazilli,"
he said, as if they were already home, as if

his sleeping child was curled like the zed
inside it now. Her shy brown face was circled
by darker strands and folds of hair—

"How old?" I could only try in English
and mimed the years with spreading fingers.
He flashed a loving victory sign.

And then it was night. We rattled
toward November. In blue uniform and cap,
a dusty porter haunted the passageway, rang

his bell for the stops in smaller villages.
The child, bumped from sleep, mumbled
something, I couldn't tell what. Was it

"Papa, are we home?" "We're almost there,"
I heard him say, or maybe
"Not yet, not yet, but soon."

The Postal Museum

It caught my eye in a travel guide to Prague:
the postal museum. And under glass, a penny black.
The place became a mental box to add, then

tick off of our itinerary, a bracketed aside
scribbled on the back of a postcard. But now,
except for one morning, it hasn't rained

so seems a shame to waste our daylight hours
bent over glass displays of gum arabic,
rare stamps, and postmarked envelopes.

Led by views into flagstoned markets
where spires and a fountain frame surprising facades,
we drop one notion to carry another.

There's a sudden thought; the street
turns. A door opens like memory.

Boswell by the Fire

"...he leaned forwards and very delicately prodded the fire
with the iron poker, as I was afterwards pleased to think, like
a man dipping his quill into the embers of memory that were
still hot." – Richard Holmes

I still think of those flatlands and empty horizons.
And Utrecht, its tidy squares...
The cathedral's hourly summons
boomed through the draughty walls

and dark, ancient furniture of my single room.
At tea, I ate dry biscuits from a polished tray
those first afternoons, only twenty-two
but already thinking myself old. I decided

to hate it there, but resolved to remain
through that wind-rattled winter
with a soldier's discipline: wake at six thirty,
read Ovid till nine, study Dutch and French,

then essays, lectures, and letters to friends.
In the eyes of my father I'd straighten up.
I'd make amends for an idle past,
become industrious, chaste and good,

gain favour with the Court, and sail
back to London a fine, firm gentleman.
But I was unstrung by the old problem:
girls. Their sentiments and boredoms,

their whims. And those profiles in doorways,
flushed whirls on the dance floor,
décolletage in candlelight! Do you remember
Madame Geelvinck? She was young,

beautiful, coy, and spoilt. Rich and widowed
at twenty-four. Like those many other suitors,
I slaved for her attention, lugging baskets
on errands while doting on her son, bungling

my French in hope she'd correct me.
Then she left for The Hague. On that cold day of rain,
like a soaked dog, I slunk to the sentry post
of St. Catherine's Gate, bribing the guard

with a bottle of Geneva, just to huddle
inside the door to watch her coach slip past.
Such antics, I know. And what for?
You'd said she had no passion, but held

your tongue and its easy ridicule,
and helped me drag my head-cold out
of that wet month of depression
with lessons in your realist's school

of laughter and frankness. And you.
You were bashing a shuttlecock
across a badminton net the first time we met.
Your feet shuffled and dashed within

your skirts' pleated billows. You became
my friend, and let me confide in you
as we ate desserts while playing whist at salons
and dances, even as you mocked the pretence

of society, wealth, and dull marriages (and my tailored
sea-green suit) with a grin that betrayed the gravity
of your every measured breath. It unsettled me,
that proud and heated talk of freedom, how

you goaded me against the smallest compromise
lest I regret it later. Don't just settle for anything,
you had me promise, or shadows will
harden in the angles of your face.

So, just as sudden as these first winter days,
years later, I awake from dreams
of old cities, long-lost scenes
and faces. I've been too long in London now,

where my every frustrated ambition raps
on the window glass. Is it only these December gusts?
Or my own dull spirit gnawing as on a bone
at the memories of youth, those pithy lusts

I'd been no stranger to with any Jenny or Alice
breathing in my arms. I inhale them now,
each pleasant gasp, like a decanted vintage
or *Hermippus Redivivus*. But there's a haunting face

I see though never catch, that turns away
and sinks into the shadows of a Holland
thirty summers ago. I'll not erase
nor change it now, the June I departed

through the tulip rows to seek my fame,
your familiar eyes grown suddenly awkward
as the swallows slashed along the moat
through the darkening colonnade of beeches.

"Have you ever been in love?" I asked.
"If *one* might feel a strong affection ... if *one*
might meet *un homme amiable*—" you hinted,
"and *if* those affections were *returned*, then..."

Well, it was dusk; I had to go. I took my leave
in the half-light. Madame—no longer Mademoiselle—
forgive these idle musings; it's late,
and it seems I'm tired. It feels

like time itself has dusted off these thoughts,
and fusses at my broken tooth
like a mouldering memento arranged
upon this mantel above the fire, where,

like a moth, I've come to do my stubborn dance.
I lean towards the ochre logs that scowl, hiss, and crackle—
such restrained heat—and imagine my green self
burned away in a past I cannot touch.

Rain beats the casements, and the panes' lead
chatters in the sleety wind. "Will you think of me?"
you said. That fading look, the last, returns,
in spite of thirty Junes apart. I always have.

II

Root Cellar

The latch is still black. Just
a pinch with your thumb, and you're in.
The old paint swells and flakes
with damp, though the sunk trough
along the walls where the rain
drained is dry as ash.
The pipe was cemented up
when new drainage was dug.
There's hardly any light, even
with the bulb, its string
a long thin strip off some rag,
and the one window long since
crusted with dirt. What is it
about these artificial depths
that turns the light yellow, almost
swallowing it? We're tourists
to our past for the little
we come here now, where once
the daily boot-falls
descended for potatoes, turnips
or a dry stick of wood.
Beet and relish jars were stored
where these empty shelves jut out,
level and braced on wedges, then
lined with folded newspaper.
I tear some down.
The date's survived, one from
my childhood. But no news,
just the faded weather page, its
sweeping lines and cartoon clouds.
The numbers predict tomorrow
will be cold, with a chance of rain.

The Game

The trees skitter past, a rush of verticals
at the roadside. I'm fifteen
in the rear-view, off to play
the softball tournament at Golden Lake.

There's Tommy, Trevor, and me.
And Trevor's older brother, Kevin,
who shit-grins behind the steering wheel,
getting us there for the 10 a.m. pitch.

Somewhere down these back routes,
just for kicks, he guns the rusted chassis
at rising humps in the road,
full speed, trying to jimmy us

loose from gravity, and slip
a fat envelope of air
between our wheels and the earth.
Each time we land, our tailbones jab

the vinyl seats, and the stitched gloves
jostle in our laps, their punched palms
a darker tan than last summer.
Kevin's loving the morning breeze

forced through the rolled-down windows,
but especially the looks of panic
on his passengers' faces,
as if we were clean, plush cushions

he'd been itching to knock
the stuffing from. "Watch
this," he says, pushing the gas pedal
to the dusty mat, then charges

the wrong side of the next blind hill.
Our heads are numb; our stomachs roll
and clutch. I catch my own eye
in the side mirror, giddy with the look

of death, every bit as close as it might appear.

After the Funeral

Some stay on the hill for hours,
still as the chiselled stone; others shut the doors
of cars, and drive back to their hotel, or home,
visitors

to that hill in years yet to come. And some
of us gather, as we should, to drink and bequeath
unto ourselves the memories not eclipsed
by death.

Through the candid gloom of the bar I watch you
mourning there among the faces, a hall of mirrors
lit with stories and clumsy stabs
at humour

we hope will frame and explain a life. I hold
myself in a cool remove, stubborn over beers.
Wanting, times like this, to be like you.
In tears.

The Old Story

I   At the Start

They fell into the old story,
the self-unsettling tale that begins
with a shared double-take, extends
to playful grins

whose lips become locked, whose tongues
are soon mopping mixed gin off
the muscling swirl of another sweet
tongue. Aloof,

they met again, uncertain,
but played it cool, prepared for the hurt,
so talked with their cards close
to the chest, near the heart.

Or not. Rather
called, hooked up, had sushi and laughs, cleared
a few felt naps at the pool hall,
sipped Coronas in bed.

And so, they took
the chance, didn't count on the worst, just played
for the good of the thrill, said *love's never assured,*
and let it ride.

They bowed. They
kissed the idol of the other's carved smile
with bent knees, bent necks, gladly low, embracing
the terms of self-exile

in their stark-new
colony of two. Two in a room safe from the great
alone. And spread out on their private flag—a quilt, down-filled
and white—

and they stroked
their astonished hips across the frets and cello moans
of the other. But more, they wanted to share
stuff, so made loans

of books
and CDs, said *you should listen to this,* hoping those
kindred lyrics and the pedal-steel might ring a bit true,
and expose

the stalled core
of what they might feel. Smitten, they traded quips
on old hairdos in photos, Wim Wenders, dumb secrets,
all the creeps

and dead ends
they once dated. And rushed over at the end of their shifts,
called when they couldn't, and might, for example, in a restaurant
notice a faint drift

of freckles
on the collarbone one itched to slide a fingertip over,
but mostly just wanted and wanted and wanted to be
with each other.

III   Some Questions Then

All the usual stuff.
Like what should they do with themselves? A few
fancy drinks? Out to dinner? What did they feel like?
Seafood? Tofu?

Instead, maybe stay
in, hole up with the couch, paperbacks, and some takeout.
Or blow off an evening just talking. But what,
really, about?

Who they were,
how they thought, what they wanted from life, dogged by their lack
of direction. Am I smart? Do you think I look nice? Am I
good in the sack?

Their ebony Docs
dripping slush into the boot mat, glacial clouds tossing hail
at the window as the late became *very*, them
tipping the green heel

of a second bottle
of something Aussie into the stemware, then a shiraz splat
drying in dimples of glass, olive pits greying
on a side plate,

but they that late hour
with their hearts in their stares might say, what if you stayed?
Is there room for your stuff? Would we do okay?
Or argue often?

Do you like doing dishes?
Have you read Henry James? I thought you didn't like eggplant?
For someone who claims they don't like eggplant you sure
eat a lot of eggplant.

IV   They Merged Their Lives

like furniture
in a shared apartment, the way tines
and blades of flatware in a drawer become
mismatched designs,

the difference unnoticed
until the guests arrive for dinner. But the bigger picture
was just beneath their serious talks
and playful banter,

the question of how
to stay one's self but also change inside, to float
free and still be centred in the eye of the other's
desire. A lot

to ask or have
as their separate pasts, present and future,
habits and friends, were shuffled conjointly
into a double exposure,

each of them
one half of the great good of being together. They tried,
stitched their plans and pet peeves with a length
of common thread

then spread out
on the bed to see if they'd sleep well.
Nice to have someone else to balance the sides,
or meet in the middle.

V   Met for Drinks and Talked

They sat there, the two of them, flanked
by the Crystal Palace of whiskey bottles, glassware,
and mirrors, the time-rubbed caramel
of wood. On bar-

stools, with brass, slouched in repose.
And talked, the band tuning up, but let
down by the turnout. And shot shit
on how they met,

what they'd meant when they said,
how they'd not understood, holding back
what they had to. Case study
of a love life. A wreck

is how it looked—theirs and theirs
but never really theirs. Then nothing to offer,
just sex, the letting-go factor, the inklings of trust
and commitment. Dear

Abby, the band's raw twang was
soundtrack to what's always on their minds.
Dear Willie Nelson, Dear Will Oldham. They agree
to be friends.

North Sea Music

We left the island.

The ferry's engine beat a deep
drum; the hull palmed

and slapped the crest
and trough of waves, like

a castanet's concave clap.
I hear the chant now;

something to the tune of
never, shush, never, oh, never,

never coming back.

The Throw

Throw a ball up there, into
        the open air.
Check the height, the clearing blue
        that absorbs that slight
spinning circle, stitched hourglasses
        of smudged leather pitched
into the summer's moment. In that
        curved, brief flight, whatever's
waiting to happen might. Just
        might. Love once given
could be taken back, a hitchhiker
        kidnapped, a birth, another tax hike;
the ancient glow of a collapsing star
        could reach us now
and be ignored, that scant effulgent
        pulse spent in the same blurred instant
it takes for sex to reach its peak,
        or a ball its apex.
If time were measured in distance, you've
        stood there nine hundred
million metres in the last three seconds—
        enough time for the crest
of a wave to whiten and fall, your eye
        to assess the ball,
an arm to lift, stretch, put out
        its hand, and catch.

III

I Used to Live Around Here

I used to live around here:
two rooms, one window, a year's lease.
After circling the park I'd climb the stair,
just sit, and watch the flags snap in the breeze.

We used to meet around here.
There's a part of us left in these places:
a held hand, a look, a dumb joke. A mere
sketch resists what time erases.

But I was circling your absence then,
like a climber whose base-camp is lost in snow.
It was mostly the hope of finding you again
that salvaged my humour. I see that now.

I turn away, I reach back, I let it go.
It's all I can do with that strange, scattered year.
I circle the park, climb some stairs to a window—
I used to live around here.

Café in Bodrum

Season's end. The seaside patio
is scuttled with upturned chairs.
Piped pop tunes crackle out
as the call to prayer begins.
Flags lift and drop—crescent, star,
crescent, star—as a cat yawns,
scratches its ear, squinting
from the cool earth in a terracotta pot.
Ribbons of the laid-back cooling tide
stroke the harbour wall, levelled
and listless as tourists' thoughts,
which are nowhere and everywhere.
Down market lanes, scooters
ferry hot *pide* and hack dry coughs
of grey exhaust over the interlocking stones.
No future can be delivered
so effortlessly, despite party slogans
clipped to each lamppost and awning
for the last stretch of the coming election,
though History's narrowed eye
might pause to blink
over a cloud of froth on a cappuccino
or these yacht masts jabbing the azure.
Mausolus is too far gone to care, his
pestled tomb once a Seventh Wonder.
Now a few fluted column drums
preserve the age, but only
the mind can still descend
these outlines of stairways
to pass through imagined thresholds
into some deserted notion of repose.

We keep our backs to it, as if
for leverage, and meet
the heat of the sun on our faces.

Japan Was Weird

Japan was weird.
Wasn't it? Our *apato* heated by kerosene;
flared Imperial rooflines, toy-sized election vans
squawking anthems
and slogans from mounted bullhorns

as they inched between the housing units.
I'd walk an hour each way to the library.
Its hazy interior had a section for smoking,
so I promptly spun around
and strode to the corner to get some—

when will I ever do *this* again?—
then flattened yesterday's *Tribune*
on the desk, and puffed curlicues
of Lucky Strike smoke into the air.
If time could be killed, I directed a massacre

until five forty-five and the peace you brought to evening.
Later, just before eleven, at a loose end, I whistled
through the inky side streets for a cold, machine-vended
Asahi or Kirin (that satisfied *ke-tunk*
as the can rolled into the catch-tray).

Different plans and the little money we had
left much unsaid between us. We were paralysed
by silence on the unknown future, forgetting
that being together meant everything.
I'd crossed a continent, an ocean, half of Japan

just to bob on the grey pivot of your eye
but must have seemed adrift instead.
You thought it was you I didn't need,
but that was only the fog of being young.
One day in March, I walked along the river—

spiky, beige grass, beige water, and a sad, sunken dock
like the spine of an unearthed thunder-lizard.
Someone's golden retriever bounded up the slope
toward me, frivolous with joy. I braced for the lunge
of wet paws, staggered by its love without condition.

Arriving Early

I missed the connection at Sunch'on on your birthday.
On that stark, dark platform I shuffled options: pay
for hotel, then take the first morning bus, or backtrack
the late hours home, and begin the whole trek
over from the station on the outskirts of Kwangju
the next day (but no Friday night, and no you...).

So this: shelling out just short of three digits Canadian
for a two-hour taxi ride, the price haggled down
a token discount of several thousand *won*.
I hadn't the heart or language to complain
when we'd caught but couldn't pass
the bus I should've been on, so sought solace

in the coastal road's panorama, the calm night
curved in the straining arcs of our headlights,
the red glow of the bus's tail-end swaying ahead.
When a straight stretch appeared, and my driver sped
between the cliff face and that looming side of metal
hurtling on the right, I raised one mental

middle finger as we shot across its prow,
arrowed past and out in front, untethered now
and every inch a gain on where I might have been
if I'd been back there. Paying the fare, it felt a bit Caesarean,
that surprise advance arrival, stretching my legs, pearled
out from the warmth of my fibreglass shell, into a world

I didn't expect to be waiting in. At least, not yet.
Twenty minutes ahead, I was point man, postulate,
herald to the very tidings of myself. I leaned
against your arm, and pictured my double lagging behind:

down off the bus, puzzled, alone, rattling your doorknob,
pacing the lanes while we're out on the town. Poor slob.

First

Do you remember the clattering gates
of the bakery where we worked
that summer, between wafts

of baguette and fresh coffee?
Or the bottle of vodka you drank, cold,
with pickles, through the heat of one evening?

Or the turtle called Dante having unrivalled reign
of the bathroom in the basement
where we first kissed, though I'd meant

to do it a hundred times in certain
other places, and I don't mean rooms.
Once, when I was sick and bad-tempered

with a summer head-cold, you left
a bag of St. John's Wort hanging
from the door latch. That was a first.

I poured hot water, let it steep.
It tasted like chewing a tree but showed
you cared. Another night, I lost the house key.

You insisted on summitting the sloped roof
below the back bedroom where sometimes,
more often than not, a window was left unlocked.

It wasn't and, cat-like, you turned nervous
and couldn't be coaxed back down.
So I loped between pubs in search

of my roommate's spare, out
of breath, scared that in the interlude
you'd vanish, or were never really there.

Powerboat

It was Sunday. September. Our crew
was pushing it hard for second place.
Our ears roared as the stem-post filleted

the Venice lagoon.
Then another boat kicked into the turn
and we hit their high wash. Our sponson

just pecked the wake, but hooked,
dragged, snapped and we barrel-rolled
back over front, then tacked—

a split-second aloft—
straight down, like hitting brick
at 80 mph. My mind left;

there was a high-pitched whine
like a dog's whistle, that piped on and on.
I flat-lined. Giuseppe, the medic,

got to me, wiped the blood clear,
and blew into the place where my teeth used to be.
I'd been injured before, bruised black

as an old banana, and twice broke my nose.
This was different. There's no fear,
you just know you're gone.

Someone was screaming, *She's dead, leave her,*
and there were thumps on my chest
like a fist on a tomb.

The sky fluttered, wobbled. I started to breathe.
I was nowhere; calm, happy. My team
hovered above while I flowed underneath.

And that weird whistle, the dazzling brightness.
I drifted like TV static, prickly-warm, like Epsom salts
dissolving and sifting through Giuseppe's hand.

There's one moment I remember
in all that light and clatter: I'd been lifted
into a helicopter when something cold

went from my neck to my stomach.
It was paramedics bent over
my shattered body (for all I knew kneeling to pray),

and cutting through my race overalls with a cold
pair of scissors. I remember thinking,
But it's a La Perla bra. It's expensive,

they're going to cut it off. Then they lost me again.

The Day of the Invasion

2003: the year still sounds like science fiction.

Six forty-five a.m., the radio's
programmed to rise in unwavering volume
until murmurs nudge us—like the bobbing prows
of docked pleasure boats—awake, into a room
of cream walls pouring into baseboards.

There's weather, sports, and traffic. Local
reports. One of trailer-park residents
with a lawsuit against landowner and county—who'll
fight it—over the twice-daily back-up of sewage on carpets.
Here's a rundown of the weekend music lineup.

And experts discuss action near Basra, but can't agree
on statistics of land area vs. tonnage of ordnance.
Weather again. Chance of showers, something Celsius, grey
outlook for the week, like a breadline has formed on our sense
of well-being. The primary colours of the corner-store

glow through the 24/7, where on unguinous rollers
hot dogs bake under heat lamps, and the night guy
has just restocked the Jolt Colas
in the last stretch of quiet before joggers give way
to teens released for spring break, who scud

on battle-scarred boards into dirty banks of snow
answering their cellphones with *Not much, we're
in the parking lot.* The light's on. It's a whole new
ball game; the mind's shifted into gear,
the body headed for the shower—a hot spray

of water tamping down the hair-soaped head.
And wiping it dry, paused under a cotton towel,
buzzed by the late-breaking updates, I'm prepared
for another entrance into the day, but stall.
Aware the rising steam that softens the mirror

will evaporate, with the world still stranded there.

The Late Show

Who are you? the woman says
from the TV screen. She's woken
suddenly, flustered, has bunched
the sheets in her fists,
raising a taut slope of linen

to her sternum. She's in
the crisp black-and-white of a '40s
flick, bolt upright, her hairdo
a pile of big, perfect curls
despite the recent sleep.

And here's this guy, in a suit, sharp
tie, and Brylcreemed lines of hair like
the grooves of a new LP, watching
from the foot of her bed. Some
lover, brother, murderer, friend…

—༝༝—

But you couldn't care, so switch
the channel. You'd only wanted
a fix on tomorrow's weather
for this northern coastline so far
from home. Clouds have curtained

off the moonlight; it's been pissing rain
all evening, you with backpack but no
umbrella, cooped up inside the hotel,
just affordable with shared bath
and cable. But wait,

there's something else—a science
program. You're no Oppenheimer
and couldn't tell the common cold
from a noble gas. But you watch the camera
pan into an endless tunnel

of scaffold, ducts, and beams.
As your thumb triggers the volume
on the slim remote, there's talk of subatomic particles,
why matter has mass, and what it will take
to prove a theory of the universe,

how they'll fire protons down a tunnel
at close to the speed of light
from Geneva into France and back
until they smash and leave a post-Bang
smudge on films of silicon...

—ɯ—

It's all too much. You switch it back:
the woman again. The man, concerned,
has whispered a name, and takes
her hand to calm her. He's found a chair,
about to explain the shrouded secret

of her past, how she got from there
to here, as if a self were simply that, an arc
from A to B. You've packed the cans
of beer on ice in the bathroom sink, and go
to check their progress. The metal's

frosted, but you'll wait another precious
minute. There's a handprint on the mirror, barely
a smudge. Another soul who passed here...
the same as you, once so sure of time and space
you thought you knew what travel was.

Ever

Maybe
one day we'll be together in Krakow,
we'll see.

Could we
reach Savannah by Friday, if we drove?
Maybe.

You, me,
from the streets of Samarkand to Peggy's Cove;
we'll see

Delphi,
Angkor Wat, the markets of Asia, the Louvre,
maybe

shade-trees
on the Euphrates if time is kind enough,
we'll see.

Will we
ever live in Montreal again? Maybe not, love.
Maybe.
We'll see.

NOTES

Tales from the Revolution
capo de tutti capi: "the boss of bosses"

Czarna Polewka
Black soup serves as a plot element in "Pan Tadeusz," a Polish epic poem by Adam Mickiewicz.

Boswell by the Fire
Though some of the details and tone are suggested by James Boswell's journals, this poem was inspired by Richard Holmes's essay "Boswell Among the Tulips" from his book *Sidetracks*, one among many of his very fine books. The poem's narrative and a number of the images are borrowed from that essay.

Hermippus Redivivus: a medical treatise recommending that ageing men should inhale the breath of young women

The Throw
If time were measured…: "To make manipulating spacetime a little easier, physicists have developed a trick to express measurements of space and measurements of time in the same way, using the same units. The speed of light provides the ultimate yardstick. How long does a meter last in time? Just so long as light takes to cross that distance—3.3 billionths of a second. How far is a second? It is the distance light travels in one tick of the clock, 186, 000 miles, or 300 *million* meters." – from *Einstein in Berlin,* by Thomas Levenson

Powerboat
In 1999, during the European Championship, stuntwoman and powerboat racing champion Sarah Donohue nearly died when her boat overturned at high speed. She severed her facial nerves, broke her jaw (and nearly every other bone in her body), died twice, survived a coma, and is now racing again. This poem is a paraphrase of her account in an interview about the accident.

Acknowledgments

The author wishes to thank the City of Ottawa, the Ontario Arts Council, and the Canada Council for the Arts for essential financial assistance during the writing of this book.

Much thanks to the editors of the following publications, where some of these poems first stretched their legs: *The Malahat Review, Arc Magazine, The Fiddlehead, Maissoneuve Magazine, This Magazine, The Drunken Boat* (online), *Sentinel Poetry* (online), *Dogs* (a chapbook published by the Olive Reading Series, Edmonton), and *The Echoing Years: An Anthology of Poetry from Canada and Ireland* (Waterford Institute of Technology, Ireland).

"North Sea Music" is for Struan Sinclair.

Thank you to many friends and my family. Thanks to Kitty, Don, Maureen, Alayna, and everyone at Brick Books for their continued support and attention.

Thank you to my friends Chris Swail, Robyn Guest, Andrew Farrell, Lisa Baird, and all at the Manx Pub over the years.

I owe much to Ken Babstock, as always, for his friendship and singular mind.

And I am deeply indebted to Henry Shukman, who edited this book and overwhelmed me with his generosity, honesty, dedication, and exemplary ear.

David O'Meara lives in Ottawa,
where he tends bar.